# *The Bridge of San Luis Rey*

## by Thornton Wilder

# A Study Guide by Ray Moore

**Acknowledgements:**
Thanks, as always, are due to Barbara for reading the manuscript and making many helpful suggestions, and for putting the text into the correct formats for publication. Any errors which remain are my own.

I am indebted to the work of numerous translators, biographers, and critics as I have acknowledged in the Bibliography. As always, I am very aware that I stand on the shoulders of giants. Where I am conscious of having taken an idea, or actual words, from a particular author, I have cited the source in the text. Any failure to do so is an omission which I will immediately correct if it is drawn to my attention.

Where I have selectively quoted from the writings of others in the course of my own argument, I have done so in the sincere belief that this constitutes fair use.

Thornton Wilder (1897-1975) photographed by Carl Van Vechten in 1948. This image is public domain

# Contents

# Preface

A prolific playwright and author of seven novels, Thornton Wilder (1897-1975) was both popular with the general public and highly regarded by the critical establishment of his day which heaped honors upon him. *The Bridge of San Luis Rey* is ranked 37 on the Modern Library list of the 100 best novels of the 20th century. Nevertheless, Wilder's works seem to be unfashionable today, with the notable exceptions of the play *Our Town* and the novel *The Bridge of San Luis Rey* which have both retained their popularity. The latter gets a rating of 3.8 (out of 5) stars on Goodreads with nearly 20,000 votes.

An Overview of the novel is given at the end of this Study Guide. It gives the kind of critical analysis that you might prefer not to have before reading the novel for the first time. On the other hand, some readers might prefer to read the Overview first.

## Thornton Wilder: A Timeline

1897: April 17, born in Madison, Wisconsin, the second of Amos Parker Wilder and Isabella Niven Wilder's five children.

1920: awarded Bachelor of Arts degree at Yale University.

1926: first novel, *The Cabala*, published.

1927: second novel, *The Bridge of San Luis Rey*, published.

1928: awarded the Pulitzer Prize for Fiction for *The Bridge of San Luis*.

1930-1937: taught at the University of Chicago (comparative literature and composition).

1938: awarded the Pulitzer Prize for Drama for *Our Town*.

1942: awarded the Pulitzer Prize for Drama for *The Skin of Our Teeth*.

1951-2: Professor of Poetry at Harvard.

1952: awarded the Gold Medal for Fiction by the American Academy of Arts and Letters.

1955-7: the play *The Matchmaker* ran for 486 performances on Broadway.

1963: awarded the Presidential Medal of Freedom.

1968: awarded the National Book Award for Fiction for his penultimate novel *The Eighth Day*.

1975: December 7, died in his sleep at the age 78.

# Dramatis Personae

## The Five Victims of the Bridge Collapse

**Doña María, the Marquesa de Montemayor:** The daughter of a rich merchant, Doña María is starved of love first by her parents and then by her husband. By marriage she becomes one of the great, noble ladies of Lima. Her estranged daughter, Doña Clara, marries a Spaniard and moves to Spain. Doña María visits her daughter only once, but maintains a correspondence with her which later becomes famous in Spanish literature. [The character is based on the distinguished French letter-writer Marie de Rabutin-Chantal, Madame de Sevigne (1626-1696).]

**Pepita:** A girl raised at the Convent of Santa María Rosa de la Rosas, whom Doña María takes as a companion and surrogate daughter.

**Esteban** [and **Manuel**]: Twins left at the Convent of Santa María Rosa de la Rosas as infants: They are virtually inseparable and no one can tell them apart. Manuel falls hopelessly in love with the actress Camila Perichole but gives up his passion for her. He cuts his knee on a piece of metal; it becomes infected, and he dies. Esteban falls into a deep depression.

**Uncle Pio:** An independent but cultured man who makes a living in many different ways. He buys Micaela Villegas when she is twelve and educates her to become the greatest actress in Peru, Camila Perichole.

**Don Jamie:** The son of Camila Perichole and Don Andres. He is a sickly child who is going to live with Uncle Pio at the time of their deaths.

## Characters Whose Lives were Intertwined with those of the Victims

**Brother Juniper:** A Franciscan monk who is on his way to cross the bridge when it collapses. He spends six years compiling a book which gives every detail of the lives of the five victims of the tragedy.

**The Abbess Convent of Santa María Rosa de la Rosas:** Takes a particular interest in Pepita and the twin brothers, Esteban and Manuel, all of whom are orphans raised in the convent.

**Camila Perichole (aka Micaela Villegas):** Under Uncle Pio's strict guidance she develops into the most honored actress in Lima. She becomes the mistress of the Viceroy by whom she has three illegitimate children and retires from the stage to live the life of a respectable lady. [This character is based on a later historical figure María Micaela Villegas Hurtado (1748-1819).]

**Doña Clara:** Daughter of Doña María, who marries The Conde Vincente d'Abuirre, a nobleman with great influence at the Spanish court.

**Captain Alvarado:** An adventurer who hires Esteban to sail with him just days before the bridge tragedy.

**The Catholic Archbishop of Lima:** An obese man who enjoys the company of the nobles of the city. He performs the service at the cathedral for the five accident victims.

**Don Abdres, The Viceroy:** Takes the beautiful actress Camila Perichole as his mistress. He is based on the historical figure Manuel de Amat y Juniet.

## Study Guide:

The questions are *not* designed to test you but to help you to locate and to understand characters, plot, settings, and themes in the text. They do not normally have simple answers, nor is there always one answer. Consider a range of possible interpretations - preferably by discussing the questions with others. Disagreement is to be encouraged!

### Part One: PERHAPS AN ACCIDENT
### Pre-reading

The spring of 2011 saw a succession of tornadoes (estimated at 1,475) hit the South and Midwest of the U.S.A. causing 536 deaths. The worst single incident occurred in the late afternoon of Sunday, May 22nd, 2011, when Joplin, a city of about 50,000 people in southwest Missouri, was hit by a massive tornado that cut a path through the city nearly six miles long killing 154 people. The area impacted by this devastation falls within America's 'Bible Belt' a name which reflects deep faith rooted in socially conservative evangelical Protestantism.

1. When something like this happens, it is legally referred to as an "Act of God." What does this mean?
2. Incidents like this test the faith of those who believe in an omnipotent God. (Obviously the example here relates to Christians, but this challenge to faith is certainly shared by many religions including Judaism and Islam.) What answers do ministers give to explain why good people die apparently so arbitrarily?
3. How would you personally react if something like this happened to those you loved? (Perhaps it has – a road accident, a cancer diagnosis, etc.)

### Reading

1. Why is it "unthinkable" that the bridge would break?
2. How do servant girls and usurers (money lenders) react to the deaths of the five on the bridge? Explain why.
3. Peru is a place where sudden death is common, so it is surprising that the bridge tragedy had the profound effect on people that it did. What factors explain its impact?
4. What do you understand by the term "proper control" (8) in the context of any scientific experiment? How is it that the five deaths offer Brother

Juniper the prospect of allowing "theology to take its place among the exact sciences" (7)?

5. The narrator asserts that Brother Juniper is not motivated by "skepticism" (8), meaning doubt, but by a conviction that his project will prove God's control of human life. There is, however, one hint that perhaps the monk's faith is not as secure as he believes it to be. What is the clue?

6. We learn that Brother Juniper's huge book "was publicly burned" (9). Speculate on the reason for the burning.

7. Why does Brother Juniper miss the "central passion" of the lives of each of the five victims (9)? What does the narrator mean when he says that he also may have missed "the very spring within the spring" in his account of the lives of the five victims?

8. The following quotations are referred to, either directly or implicitly, in this chapter. Link each one to the text.

a) *The blind poet Milton sets out the thesis of his greatest work:*

> What in me is dark
> Illumine, what is low raise and support;
> That to the height of this great argument
> I may assert eternal Providence,
> And **justify the ways of God to men**.
> (John Milton, *Paradise Lost*, Book One, Lines 22-26)

*Pope does the same for what is his greatest poem:*

> Let us (since Life can little more supply
> Than just to look about us and to die)
> Expatiate free o'er all this scene of Man;
> A mighty maze! but not without a plan; …
> Laugh where we must, be candid where we can;
> But **vindicate the ways of God to Man**.
> (Alexander Pope, *Essay On Man*, Epistle One, Lines 3-16)

b) *Macbeth is contemplating the murder of King Duncan in Shakespeare's play:*

> Besides, this Duncan
> Hath borne his faculties so meek, hath been
> So clear in his great office, that his virtues
> Will plead like angels, trumpet-tongued, against
> The deep damnation **of his taking-off**;
> (William Shakespeare, Macbeth, Act 1 Scene 7 Lines 16-20)

5

c) *Gloucester reflects on man's helplessness in Shakespeare's play:*

> I' th' last night's storm I such a fellow saw,
> Which made me think a man a worm. My son
> Came then into my mind, and yet my mind
> Was then scarce friends with him. I have heard more
> since. **As flies to wanton boys are we to th' gods.**
> **They kill us for their sport.**
> (William Shakespeare, *King Lear*, Act 4 Scene 1 Lines 32-7)

d) *Jesus promises his disciples that God holds their fate in his hands:*

> Are not two sparrows sold for a farthing? and **one of them shall not**
> **fall on the ground without your Father.**
> But the very hairs of your head are all numbered.
> Fear ye not therefore, ye are of more value than many sparrows.
> (*Gospel of Matthew*, 10: 29-31, King James Version)

*Horatio urges Hamlet to follow the 'bad feeling' he has about a proposed*
*fencing match in Shakespeare's play:*

> Horatio:
> If your mind dislike any thing, obey it. I will forestall their
> repair hither, and say you are not fit.
> *Hamlet:*
> Not a whit, we defy augury. **There is special providence in**
> **the fall of a sparrow.** If it be now, 'tis not to come; if it be not to
> come, it will be now; if it be not now, yet it will come—the
> readiness is all. Since no man, of aught he leaves, knows what is't
> to leave betimes, let be.
> (William Shakespeare, *Hamlet*, Act 5 Scene 2 Lines 217-224)

9. What is significant about the title of this chapter?

**Post-reading**

The narrator writes that Brother Juniper is in Peru and present at the moment the Bridge of San Luis Rey collapses because of "a series of coincidences so extraordinary that one almost suspects the presence of some Intention" (p. 6). This raises the central question of the novel: Does man live out his life in a universe given meaning by the Intentions of God, or in a universe which is arbitrary and random because there is no God? Since the narrator criticizes Juniper's book for its failure to convey the essence of each of the five victims, it clearly was not the book itself which was the reason for his presence. As you read, the novel you should ask what other Intention God might have had for placing Brother Juniper at the scene.

The bridge itself is a symbol of human life: we travel from birth to death at each point holding onto life by a thread which might break at any moment. As the bridge goes down, the five people thrown from it are described as "five gesticulating ants" (7). This image stresses how insignificant and vulnerable each human life is compared with the valley into which they fall, the earth, and the universe. Doña María will have a similar feeling when confronted by the Andes near the end of Part 2 (35).

## Part Two: THE MARQUESA DE MONTEMAYOR

### Reading

1. In what ways have biographers distorted the truth about Doña María, the Marquesa de Montemayor? What has led them to do so?
2. What is wrong with the way in which Doña María loves her daughter, Doña Clara?
3. Doña María's letters are acknowledged to be literary masterpieces. What motivates her to write them so carefully?
4. What farcical misunderstanding results from Camila Perichole's mockery of Doña María during her visit to the theater?
5. The Perichole is forced by the Viceroy (whose mistress she is) to visit Doña María in order to apologize for her behavior at the theater. What entirely unexpected reaction does the Perichole experience when she meets Doña María? How does their relationship develop during the meeting?
6. What plans does the Abbess have for Pepita?
7. What is lacking emotionally in Pepita's life?
8. During her preparations for Doña Clara's child-birth, in what ways does Doña María's religious faith develop?
9. Why is Doña María's death at the time that it happens particularly tragic? Why is the death of Pepita in its way equally tragic?

### Post-reading

Doña María is starved of love as a child. When she has a child of her own, she focuses all of her love on it, but in a way that is ultimately selfish. The child, Clara, resents being manipulated and does not return her mother's love. As an orphan, Pepita has also been starved of love. Her surrogate mother, the Abbess, is so busy educating her to take over her official position that she does not show her love for the young girl. Doña María becomes another surrogate mother, but only occasionally does she show the young girl affection and consideration. However, in the days immediately before their deaths, the two begin to understand the failure of their lives and are ready to change.

Although neither of them is aware of it, Doña María has much in common with Camila Perichole, for both are absorbed in that falsifying of emotion which is acting. Doña María's 'stage' is her letters where she strains to create effects which will win the approval of her daughter. Significantly,

## *The Bridge of San Luis Rey* by Thornton Wilder

Doña María teaches Camila Perichole a gesture which comes straight from her imaginary relationship with her daughter.

Having learned from Pepita's letter what honest, generous love really is, Doña María re-writes what turns out to be her last letter to her daughter. Wilder says history remembers Letter LVI as the Marquesa's "Second Corinthians." Many critics believe that Wilder actually had in mind 1st Corinthians 13: 4-8:

> Love is patient, love is kind. It does not envy, it does not boast, it is not proud.  It is not rude, it is not self-seeking, it is not easily angered, it keeps no record of wrongs.  Love does not delight in evil but rejoices with the truth. It always protects, always trusts, always hopes, always perseveres. Love never fails. But where there are prophecies, they will cease; where there are tongues, they will be stilled; where there is knowledge, it will pass away.

## Part Three: ESTEBAN

### Reading

1. Why is it that the Abbess is not able to truly love the twins?
2. What aspects of the twins' love for each other are presented critically in the narrative?
3. What is wrong with the 'love' that Manuel feels for Camila Perichole?
4. How does Esteban react when his brother dies? Why does he take Manuel's name?
5. What experience of life unites the Abbess and Captain Alvarado with Esteban?
6. How is Esteban saved from the depression into which he has sunk? (Look for the lie that the Captain tells him on page 67 and ask yourself why he lies.) Why is Esteban 's death tragic?

### Post-reading

The twins Manuel and Esteban grow up isolated from the rest of the world by their orphan status and by the unique bond which they share as twins. They have a love for each other which does not need language. Even though they have their own private language, words are still to them an inferior form of communication. Whilst both the Marquesa and the Perichole rely on words to generate emotion, the twins know that words cannot produce emotion; they can only express emotion that is already present.

The first separation between the two happens when Manuel falls in hopelessly love with the Camila Perichole. Following his brother's death from an infected leg wound, Esteban adopts Manuel's name for a time and isolates himself in his grief. The Abbess, however, succeeds in engaging Captain Alvarado to recruit Esteban for his next voyage; Esteban is going to meet the ship when he is killed. We learn that both the Abbess and the Captain have suffered losses comparable to that of Esteban, and together they help him to understand that life means going on.

## *The Bridge of San Luis Rey* by Thornton Wilder

## Part Four: UNCLE PIO

### Reading

1. Just before the description of his discovery of the girl whom he will form into Camila Perichole, the narrator points out two sources of unhappiness/failure in Uncle Pio's life. Explain them.

2. Uncle Pio and Camila Perichole are said to love one another (83), but what is wrong with this love? How is the weakness in their love for each other similar to the weakness in the love of Esteban and Manuel?

3. In what ways does the relationship between Uncle Pio and Camila Perichole resemble, and in what ways does it differ from, those of the Marquesa and her daughter and of Esteban and Manuel?

4. Explain why Camila Perichole cuts herself off from everyone following the loss of her beauty due to small-pox.

5. Why is Uncle Pio's death at the time that it happens particularly tragic? Why is the death of Don Jamie in its way also tragic?

### Post-reading

In his youth, Uncle Pio shows the same restlessness and the same independence as do Esteban and Manuel, "He never did one thing for more than two weeks at a time even when enormous gains seemed likely to follow upon it" (79).

## Part Five: PERHAPS AN INTENTION

### Reading

1. Why is Brother Juniper's friend, the master at the University of San Martín, bitterly convinced that "all was wrong with the world" (111)?

2. What does Brother Juniper's comparison of the relative worth of the victims and the survivors of an epidemic prove?

3. What impact does the bridge tragedy have upon the main surviving characters: Madre María, Camila Perichole, and Doña Clara?

4. Explain the title of Part Five and its final sentence.

### Post-reading

The novel's denouement is deliberately ambiguous. Critics disagree on its effectiveness. Castronovo calls it "clumsy and sentimental," while Goldstein says that it is "not sentimental; it offers no promises of earthly rewards and no overestimation of the worth of characters."

*The Bridge of San Luis Rey* by Thornton Wilder

# Study Guide: Suggested Answers

The answers provided do not pretend to be final and definitive. They are provided as suggestions for students and teachers who want to be sure that they are thinking on the right lines.

## Part One: PERHAPS AN ACCIDENT

### Pre-reading

1. An Act of God is a legal term for events beyond the power of humans to control, such as sudden floods, earthquakes and other natural disasters, for which no one can be held guilty or liable.

2. Christian ministers have a variety of responses, including:
   a) God is punishing the individuals who died for their sins;

   b) God is punishing a whole society for its ills - all individuals are members of society, so all are guilty (compare Sodom and Gomorrah);

   c) God's purpose is unknowable - man's function is to have faith not to question God;

   d) The dead have gone to a better place - God has taken them to himself.

   [Did I miss any?]

### Reading

1. It is protected by the name of a French king who was also a saint and by the small mud church at one end.

2. Servant girls give back things they have stolen, and money lenders try to justify their charging of interest on loans (which the Catholic Church regarded as the sin of usury). Each set of people has been reminded that they might be called to Judgment at any moment.

3. Probably because such accidents were usually on a huge scale and therefore anonymous. These five people were well known individuals. Also, everyone in Lima knew that it could have been them who died.

4. "Proper control" means that a science experiment actually tests the thing that it sets out to test. By excluding the possibility that a reaction or an effect can be caused by any other influence, the experiment is valid because it gives the same result every time it is performed. Brother Juniper begins from the principle the collapse of the bridge was clearly an 'Act of God' and not, for example, a piece of negligence. Therefore, God must

13

have had a reason for doing it. If there are thousands of victims (of an earthquake perhaps), it is clearly not possible to trace the reasons for the death of all those people, but five is an ideal number - provided that in each case a reason can be demonstrated.

5. He remembers times when his prayers seemed to bring rain, but even more "times when weeks went by" before it rained (9). He dismisses that thought because he senses that even to think about the failure of prayer is to acknowledge doubt.

6. From the clues in this chapter, it seems that the book did not actually prove what it set out to prove. Heretics (i.e. those who maintain religious opinions contrary to those of the Church) are burned, so perhaps the book was pronounced heretical. Of course, that would also mean that Brother Juniper would be burned as a heretic.

7. Brother Juniper was not trying to find out about the five victims as people. To him they were simply "specimens" in a "laboratory" (7). The narrator might also fail, not because he did not try, but because each of us is ultimately unknowable to someone else.

8.
   a) These two quotes express the aim of Brother Juniper's investigation which is to prove that "we live by plan and die by plan" (7). He aims to "justify the ways of God to man" (8).
   b) Brother Juniper sets out to find the reason for the apparently random deaths, the "taking off" (7), of the five people who fell from the bridge.
   c) and d) These three quotations are referenced in the last sentence (10). They represent the two ways of looking at why 'bad stuff happens': either the gods are playing with us to take joy in our suffering, or God is in control and does everything for a purpose.

9. Brother Juniper, and presumably everyone else in Lima, regarded the bridge tragedy as an 'Act of God,' but what if it was just an accident? That would mean that we live in a random, meaningless universe, with no God in control.

## Part Two: THE MARQUESA DE MONTEMAYOR

1. The biographers assume that because she wrote such beautiful letters, Doña María must have been personally attractive and gracious. In fact, she was ugly, introverted, drank too much, and was basically a laughing stock in Lima. Hers was a sad life.

2. Doña María's love for her daughter, Doña Clara, is described as "idolatrous," that is, she loves her daughter for what she wants her to be not for herself. As a result, there is nothing but conflict between the two because Clara resists her mother's attempts to remake her to conform to her image of the daughter she wants her to be. Doña María desperately wants her daughter to return the love that she has for her, but this reveals the essential weakness of Doña María's love, "she loved her daughter not for her daughter's sake, but for her own" (18). Essentially, Doña María's love is purely selfish.

3. Doña María's letters are a desperate attempt to get from her daughter, if not a show of love for her, at the least some admiration., "she wanted to hear her [daughter] say, 'You are the best of all possible mothers'; she longed to hear her whisper, 'Forgive me'" (19). The letters are a desperate attempt to "attract the attention, perhaps the admiration, of her distant child" (16). Thus, she composes carefully, writing many drafts hoping to discover phrases "that might bring a smile to her daughter's face and might make her murmur: 'Really, my mother is charming'" (23). Ironically, Doña María's attempts to "dazzle her daughter" (17) come to nothing because Clara merely skims them. It is her husband who finds them delightful and who preserves them for posterity.

4. In the interval of the play, it is the Perichole's custom to entertain the audience with improvised topical songs. On this occasion, she makes Doña María the subjects of her satirical songs "alluding to her appearance, her avarice, her drunkenness, and even to her daughter's flight from her" (22). Doña María is, however, abstracted and does not perceive that she is being mocked and laughed at by the audience. It is Pepita who drags her away from the theater to protect her from the pain of the attacks.

5. The Perichole visits Doña María with the expectation that she will go through the motions of making an apology but not mean it. In the event, Doña María carries herself with such distinction that the Perichole "was struck for the first time with the dignity of the old woman" (25). As a

result of the misunderstanding at the theater, when the Perichole comes to make her apology, Doña María has not the faintest idea what she is apologizing for since she remembers the play as having been delightful and cannot remember clearly why she had to leave early. The Perichole cannot believe that the old woman did not understand her insulting songs and concludes that she is acting "out of a sort of fantastic magnanimity" so that a "piercing sense of shame filled her" (26). For the first time in her life, someone shows Doña María love as the Perichole kisses her hand and speaks of her goodness. This gives Doña María the opportunity to unburden herself about her failed relationship with her daughter. She even thinks for a moment that she is talking to Doña Clara calling her "'my daughter'" (27).

6. The Abbess is a feminist centuries before feminism was possible. She has "fallen in love with an idea several centuries before its appointed appearance in the history of civilization" (29-30). She has found in Pepita a woman who does not depend on the love of a man for her self-image and, aware that she is herself getting old, has begun to groom the girl as her successor.

7. As an orphan, Pepita has never known love, "She had never been taught to expect happiness" (32). Sometimes Doña María talks to her and shows her consideration, but then she withdraws into herself so that, "The beginnings of hope and affection that Pepita had such need to expend would be wounded" (33).

8. Doña María knows how dangerous child-birth can be. It seems to her that humans are "in the hands of malignant Nature" (34). She collects all of the knowledge that she can, both pagan and Christian to help her daughter, but she is increasingly overcome by the feeling that the "world had no plan in it" (35). However, she retains faith in what she calls the "great Perhaps" (35). Faced, however, by the massive Andes, she loses her faith in the power of men and their gods to influence circumstances, "'She was listening to the new tide of resignation that was rising within her. Perhaps she would learn in time to permit both her daughter and her gods to govern their own affairs" (36).

9. Doña María has found "the new tide of resignation" (36). She has given up her attempts to manage the fate of her daughter by trying to influence God and has instead decided to leave everything in his hands. It is for this reason that when she reads a letter in which Doña Clara has made

"wounding remarks," she does not react negatively but merely places them in her heart "carefully wrapped in understanding and forgiveness" (37). Just at this point, she reads Pepita's letter to the Abbess in which the servant girl reaches out to the only mother she has ever known. At first, Doña María feels "envy" because "she longed to command another's soul as completely as this nun was able to do" (39), but when Pepita tells her that she will not send the letter because it is not "brave," Doña María has an epiphany: she suddenly realizes that, "She had never brought courage to either life or love" (41). Doña María determines to "begin a new life," and the first sign of it is the letter she writes to her daughter in which, for the first time in her life, she presents her love as generous and positive not demanding and manipulative.

The case of Pepita is similar. Madre María del Pilar has "abused" the girl's love for her by trying to mould her in her own image, so that Pepita felt only discipline and not love (38). Pepita is taking the first steps to express her love for "the only real thing in her life," but is cut off before she can make human contact with Madre María (38).

## Part Three: ESTEBAN

1. The Abbess grows "fond" of the twins when they are children, and this fondness develops into 'love' (46). However, Madre María "had come to hate all men" (46), and so as the boys grow into their teens, she "would catch herself gazing deep into their black and frowning eyes, looking for those traits that would appear when they grew to be men, all that ugliness, all that soullessness, that made hideous the world she worked in" (46-7). Notice that she perceives their eyes as "black and frowning" which tells us more about her than it does about them. Madre María sees it as inevitable that the young boys will grow into evil men. Thus, when they become old enough to arouse the sexual interest of the nuns, the twins are moved out of the convent. This is why Madre María is not able to love the twins.

2. The weakness of the love between Esteban and Manuel is its very strength. The two are inseparable and they are indistinguishable: it is as though they are one person. Thus, when the Archbishop tries to discover the meaning of their secret language, the experience is "horrible to them. They bled" (47). This suggests that they are so involved in each other that they cannot relate to society. The narrator tells us, "*love* is inadequate to describe the tacit almost ashamed oneness of these brothers ... And yet side by side with this there existed a need for one another so terrible that it produced miracles ..." (47-8). The fatal weakness of their attachment is shown when Manuel falls in 'love' with Camila Perichole. For Esteban, their life together has always been "full enough for him," so that when Manuel allows another human to enter his imagination "the whole meaning had gone out of their life" (50), and, "He seemed to shrink into space, infinitely tiny, infinitely unwanted" (54). He is shattered by the discovery that he loves Manuel more than Manuel loves him; he cannot cope with what the narrator calls "that secret from which no one every quite recovers" (50).

3. Manuel's 'love' for the actress Camila Perichole is based on her beauty: he falls in love with her without even knowing her, attracted by her "red stockings and shoes" (49). The attraction is not simply sexual, for both twins have had many sexual encounters with women without becoming emotionally involved. Manuel is not even deflected in his love by writing letters to Camila Perichole's two lovers, the Viceroy and an anonymous bullfighter. Manuel is said to worship the actress (55) who clearly has no feelings for him at all. Only when he realizes how much Esteban is hurt by his relationship with the actress does he see that beside his love for his

brother "all the other attachments in the world were shadows, or the illusions of fever" (55). Manuel gives up Camila Perichole because his love for his brother cannot include love for another.

4. Esteban becomes a "half-demented boy" following his brother's death (64). He loses the will to live, the will to accept help, the will to take a place in society. He takes Manuel's name partly because he feels guilty that he caused his brother to give up the woman he loved and that this caused his death. In a way, Esteban is 'killing' himself as punishment for murdering his own brother.

5. Madre María tells Esteban, "'I, too, Manuel have lost. I too ... once. We know that God has taken them into His hands ...'" (63). We learn no more about who died, except that the Abbess uses the plural. Captain Alvarado, we learn from one of Doña María's letters to her daughter, *had a daughter ... We have no way of knowing if she was more beautiful or intelligent than the thousands of other girls that lived about him, but she was his*" (65-6). He now travels the world to fill up the remainder of his time, and because it is easier to believe that when he returns his daughter will be in Peru all grown up.

6. When Madre María tries to persuade Esteban to see the body of his dead brother, he refuses. She reminds him of how "'as children you did so many things for me'" (63). She is trying to make Esteban see that his life has value, but she fails. It is she who talks to Captain Alvarado about Esteban. He makes progress because he is the first person whom Esteban tells his real name since his brother's death. Strangely, the Captain asks him about his brother and says that he wants to recruit him also. He must, however, know that Manuel is dead because he has talked to Madre María (65). The lie that he does not know of Manuel's death is a ruse to make Esteban admit that his brother is dead and it succeeds (67). We learn that Esteban has sought death by running into a burning building (68). He vacillates several times about agreeing to go on the Captain's next voyage, but he is prompted to respond by the desire to offer Madre María some comfort for the loss she has suffered, "'I want to give her a present ... She had a serious loss once ... Women can't bear that kind of thing like we can'" (69). For the first time since his brother's death, Esteban is thinking about someone else. After his final decision to go on the voyage, the Captain explains how he has continued to live despite his loss, "'We do

what we can. We push on, Esteban, as best we can. It isn't for long, you know. Time keeps going by. You'll be surprised at the way time passes'" (71). Having understood this, Esteban is killed when the bridge falls.

## Part Four: UNCLE PIO

1. For all of his successful money-making activities, Uncle Pio is never rich. It is as though "he abandoned a venture when it threatened to prosper" (82). Also, he is lonely, though he takes pride in his loneliness "as though there resided a certain superiority in such a solitude" (82).

2. In the early days, the relationship between Uncle Pio and Camila Perichole is almost perfect. He treats her well and she enjoys being taught and set to learn. It is said that "They loved one another deeply but without passion" (83) which means that they were not sexually involved with each other. However, Uncle Pio strives only for artistic perfection and teaches her to strive for it too, so that they end up "tormenting themselves" in the desire to attain the unattainable in the real world (86). Problems begin when Camila "lost some of this absorption in her art ... [and a] certain intermittent contempt for acting made her negligent" (86). She discovers that the audience does not notice when her performance lacks sincerity.

3. The relationship between Uncle Pio and Camila has the same inequality as that between the twins when Manuel falls in love with the actress. Uncle Pio has created a woman who is "incapable of establishing any harmony between the claims of her art, her appetites, of her dreams, and of her crowded daily routines" (88). In contrast, to Uncle Pio, Camila is "the great secret and reason of his life" (93). This recalls the essentially selfish love which Doña María has for her daughter Doña Clara. Just as Doña María's love exists only in her imagination and in the fiction and affectation of her letters, so Uncle Pio's love for Camila exists only in his imagination and on the stage. She tells him, "'There is no such thing as that kind of love and that kind of island. It is in the theater that you find such things'" (100). The bottom line is that none of these four people has a love which exists in or could ever survive in the real world.

4. Once small-pox has taken her beauty, Camila Perichole retires from public life and goes to live in her villa in the hills. She returns all former gifts and refuses to see those who come to see her. The reason is that she assumes that these people were only attached to her because of her beauty: she cannot believe that they ever loved her as a person, or that they could do so now. She believes that their visits "spring from a pity full of condescension" and she refuses to see them (102). The narrator explains, "This assumption that she need look for no more devotion now that her beauty had passed proceeded from the fact that she has never realized any

love save love as passion" (102). She cannot believe that anyone might love her unselfishly. She is reduced to the same sort of "jealous solitude" which characterized Uncle Pio's life before he met her (102). This is because she is obsessed by, "A great pain ... at her heart, the pain of a world that is meaningless" (106).

5. In having Don Jamie for a year, Uncle Pio is given a second chance to love someone. He tells Camila Perichole, "'I shall love him and take every care of him'" (106). Perhaps this time he will not make the same mistakes that he made in teaching the boy's mother. On Don Jamie's part, he is given the chance to become a part of society from which his mother has cut herself off. As he is carried towards the bridge he feels "shame ... that one of those moments was coming that separated him from other people" because of his delicate health (107), but it is precisely Uncle Pio's aim to make him feel comfortable amongst others. The accident ends that possibility.

*The Bridge of San Luis Rey* by Thornton Wilder

## Part Five: PERHAPS AN INTENTION

1. Brother Juniper's friend, the master at the University of San Martín, is bitterly convinced that "all was wrong with the world" (111) because his wife ran away to follow a soldier leaving him with two children. He does not believe in a "guided world" (112). He tells the story of a Queen whose entire people prayed that she should recover from a cancer, but she did not. He also tells of having researched the glowing epitaph of a woman on a tomb in Lima Cathedral in order to prove that those who cut the inscription in stone were lying about her goodness. He is convinced that "'in the world we do nothing but feed our wills'" (114), and that selflessness and disinterestedness are merely myths or worse lies. However, having researched the woman's life, he found the epitaph to be fully justified. This amazes him, but he will not accept that such goodness can exist on earth and concludes that "'what I said was true. The woman was an exception, perhaps an exception'" (114).

2. Brother Juniper's comparison of the victims and the survivors of an epidemic prove that "the dead were five times more worth saving [than those who lived]" (113). Thus, the facts do not support faith, so he destroys the data because it causes "a resignation that he did not permit his reason to examine" (113).

3. Madre María comes to understand "it was enough to work ... [that] it seemed sufficient for Heaven that for a while in Peru a disinterested love had flowered and faded" (117). That is, she is reconciled to the impermanence of life. She learns that she has not really allowed herself to show her love because she has been too concerned with her legacy.
Camila Perichole learns to express the love she felt for Uncle Pio and her son Don Jamie. Her "long despair ... found its rest on that dusty friendly lap [of Madre María]" (120).

Doña Carla, the Condessa d'Abuirre, learns to express her love for her mother Doña María of whom she makes "a long passionate defense" (121). She will help the Abbess with her work for they both now know, "'anywhere you may expect grace'" (121).

Above all, each of them (even Captain Alvarado) knows that life is short, but that it is enough, "soon we shall die and all memory of those five will have left the earth, and we ourselves shall be loved for a while and forgotten but that love will have been enough ..." (123).

4. Having spent the whole of the novel tracing Brother Juniper's conclusions that the fall of the bridge killed people just at the moment when they were about to begin a new life and that therefore it illustrates that we live in a directionless universe, the narrator now raises the possibility that good came of it. We are asked, "where are sufficient books to contain the events that would not have been the same without the fall of the bridge?" (120). The novel does not answer the question which Brother Juniper set out to answer: it leaves us with an ambiguous 'perhaps.'

Given that we cannot know if there is a God, the narrator suggests that we should base our lives on something that we *do know* to exist: love. Love is the only thing that gives positive meaning; it is the only thing that we know survives death. That it does not do so for very long (because time wipes away every memory) does not negate its truth and power.

**Inca Bridge Illustration:** Ponte sull'Apurimac, artist Squire, 1845. (This image is public domain. Wikimedia Commons.)

# Overview

*The Bridge of San Luis Rey* is a work of fiction. The bridge collapse in Lima, Peru, at noon on Friday, July 20, 1714, never happened, although it is a perfectly plausible invention. The bridge in the novel "is based on the great Inca road suspension bridge across the Apurímac River, erected around 1350, still in use in 1864" (Wikipedia). Wilder did not visit Peru before writing this novel.

# The Bottom Line:

Brother Juniper's investigation into the lives of the five victims, intended to reinforce faith by proving that the end of a person's life is all part of God's plan for that person, has the opposite effect. What he discovers is that each of those who die has sought love and fulfillment in their lives but that each has (in his or her own different way) failed to reach their goals. However, each is beginning life afresh on the day that they die. Thus, their deaths make no sense. For this reason, both Juniper and his book are found heretical and both are burned in the public square. However, the reader also learns that their deaths in the bridge tragedy inspire some of those who they leave behind to a more meaningful life. Thus, the novel is deliberately ambiguous about whether the fall of the bridge is a random accident or an example of divine intention.

# Themes

Normally, it is possible to list a number of different themes in a work of fiction, but in the case of this short novel everything is a variation on one theme: the quest to understand the nature of human life, mortality, and the existence (or not) of a divine will. This alerts us to the fact that this is a **philosophical novel**. As Russell Banks writes in the Foreword to *The Bridge of San Luis Rey:*

> One merely has to consider the central question raised by the novel, which, according to Wilder himself, was simply: "Is there a direction and meaning in the lives beyond the individual's own will?" It is perhaps the largest and most profoundly personal philosophical inquiry that we can undertake. It is the question that defines us as human beings. (*Wilder*)

If Banks is right in arguing that the novel is "as close to perfect a moral fable as we are ever likely to get in American literature" (*Wilder*), then it needs to be added that it is a fable which does not explicitly have a moral. Wilder himself wrote that:

> God's love has to transcend his just retribution. But in my novel I have left this question unanswered. As I said earlier, we can only pose the question correctly and clearly, and have faith one will ask the question in the right way. (Thornton Wilder)

The reader is left to decide for him/herself. Wilder commented wryly on this freedom when he told an interviewer:

> Many assured me that *The Bridge of San Luis Rey* was a satisfying demonstration that all the accidents of life were overseen and harmonized in providence; and a society of atheists in New York wrote me that it was the most artful exposure of shallow optimisms since *Candide* and asked me to address them. (*The Paris Review*)

**Coincidence** plays such a dominant role in the narrative that even the narrator is driven to speculate that the events recorded are *not* coincidental at all but the work of "some Intention," that is of a controlling deity. The most obvious examples of *apparent* coincidence are: the similarities in life-experience between the five randomly assembled victims of the bridge collapse. Five people step onto the San Luis Bridge at the same time: with the exception of two, they are entirely unknown to each other. They are, however, united by the fact that each has sought love in his/her life but has been denied it; each is in the process of trying to find the love that has evaded them. The other *apparent* coincidence is that the accident is witnessed by Brother Juniper who is perhaps the only man who could have undertaken to investigate, interpret and chronicle the event.

On the other hand, the **absurd** accident that kills five 'innocent' people raises the question of whether human lives are controlled by an all-powerful and loving God or are rather the result of purely random forces. The writer Albert Camus defined the absurd as the mismatch in an individual's consciousness between the *assumptions* upon which he/she has been living life and the *reality* of that life. Thus, the absurd rests neither in the world (which is irrational and random) nor in humans (who have an inherent need to find meaning), but rather in the *confrontation* or *interface* between the "unreasonable silence of the world" and man's "wild longing for clarity" and order (*The Myth of Sisyphus* 28 and 21). This is precisely the dilemma raised by the collapse of the bridge.

## The Bridge of San Luis Rey by Thornton Wilder

Brother Juniper, as a man of **faith**, is convinced that God must have purpose behind His decisions, and that (being a benevolent God) He must inevitably favor the worthy people over the unworthy. If this is so, then the Brother is convinced that he should be able to measure, and thus demonstrate objectively, the influence of Divine Will upon human life. Before he witnesses the bridge collapse, he has been testing this hypothesis using a scale for measuring abstract moral values such as piety and goodness, and applying the scale both to people who have suffered from tragedy and those who have not. However, he has been unable to confirm his hypothesis. In fact, his research has tended to show that the unworthy have done better in life than the worthy by a ratio of five to one.

The deaths of just five individuals appears to offer the ideal opportunity to use **scientific methods** to answer the question, "Why did this thing happen to those five people?" and to determine finally whether "we live by accident and die by accident, or we live by plan and die by plan" (7). He sets out an intellectual quest to prove that the deaths were the product of divine intervention. However, six years of research compiling vast amounts of data on these victims leaves the Brother unable to point to any moral fault that would mark these individuals for Divinely inspired tragedy. He is reduced to providing the required generalized orthodox conclusion that the fall of the bridge exemplified "pride and wealth confounded as an object lesson to the world, and humility crowned and rewarded for the edification of the city" (101). As punishment, Brother Juniper is excommunicated by the Church and burned for writing a book which set out to "justify the ways of God to man" (8) and failed to do so.

Not only is Brother Juniper's scientific inquiry fruitless, but ironically he never lives to see that the deaths of the five do bring forth the **love** that was lacking in their lives. Having lost Uncle Pio and her son, Camila Perichole dedicates herself to the convent as a volunteer aiding the Abbess in her charity work; Doña Clara, who ignored her mother during her life, sails from Spain to mourn her passing; and the Abbess of the Convent of Santa Maria Rosa de la Rosas, having witnessed the change in these two, understands the importance of human love even "soon we shall die and all memory of those five will have left the earth, and we ourselves shall be loved for a while and forgotten."

# Narrative Perspective

In *The Bridge of San Luis Rey*, Wilder uses an unidentified first-person narrator who claims to have a wider understanding of the story than Brother Juniper was able to have. However, this narrator makes no claims to be omniscient. He is all too aware that there is always an ambiguity in matters of human character and theology.

## Symbolism:

The bridge a powerful symbol of the short span and the precarious nature of human life, and of the arbitrariness, even the malevolence, of fate.

# Essay Questions:

1. The literary critic Rex J. Burbank argues that the narrative voice in *The Bridge of San Luis Rey* is a "weakness," objecting to "the sometimes obtrusive presence of the omniscient author, who judges and interprets as he narrates the histories and inner lives of the main characters."
Does the novel portray Brother Juniper's quest to prove God's plan to be noble or foolish? Analyze and evaluate Wilder's use of the narrator in the novel.
2. What is the narrator's conclusion about whether the collapse of the bridge was an accident, or the result of an intention?
3. The dominant theme of the novel love. What different forms of love can be found in the novel? Does the novel have a message about what constitutes true love?
4. Wilder wrote, "It seems to me that my books are about: what is the worst thing that the world can do to you, and what are the last resources one has to oppose it." How does this statement apply to this novel?
5. Imagine that one of the five who died in the accident survived. In fictional form, tell the story of that person's subsequent life (or any portion of that life that you choose).

## Works Cited

Wikipedia contributors. "The Bridge of San Luis Rey." *Wikipedia, The Free Encyclopedia*. Wikipedia, The Free Encyclopedia, 15 Jan. 2014. Web. 17 Mar. 2014.

"*The Bridge of San Luis Rey*." *Wilder: The Official Website of the Thornton Wilder Family*. The Wilder Family. Web. 24 Jan. 2016.

Goldstone, Richard H. "Thornton Wilder, The Art of Fiction No. 16." *The Paris Review* (1956). *The Paris Review*. Web. 24 Jan. 2016.

# READING QUIZES

## Reading Quiz - Part One: PERHAPS AN ACCIDENT

1. The Bridge of St. Louis Rey was built by:

    a) Spaniards
    b) Aztecs
    c) Incas
    d) Portuguese

2. The bridge carried:

    a) pedestrians and horses but not carriages
    b) pedestrians and horses and carriages
    c) pedestrians only
    d) pedestrians and people carried in chairs

3. The fall of the bridge is said to have impacted the behavior of all of the following *except*:

    a) usurers
    b) noble women
    c) servant girls

4. Brother Juniper is a monk of which order?

    a) Dominican
    b) Cistercian
    c) Franciscan
    d) Augustinian

5. Brother Juniper's first thought when he sees the bridge collapse was, "Within ten minutes myself ..."

    a) true
    b) false

6. How many years does Brother Juniper spend compiling his book on the lives of the victims?

    a) three
    b) five
    c) six
    d) eight

7. Which of the following is more accurate?

a) the book is burned, but Brother Juniper has a copy which he keeps hidden

b) the book is burned with Brother Juniper but a secret copy is found later

c) the book is torn up by Brother Juniper and the pieces thrown into the sea

## Reading Quiz - Part Two: THE MARQUESA DE MONTEMAYOR

1. Which of the following most accurately and completely reflects the view of the narrator?

    a) Brother Juniper fails to understand Doña María as well as her biographers do

    b) Brother Juniper understands Doña María better than do her biographers

    c) both Brother Juniper and her biographers fail to understand Doña María

2. The narrator calls Doña María a "wonderful woman" (14) for all of the following reasons *except*:

    a) she is beautiful and cultured

    b) she learns how to love her daughter

    c) she writes wonderful letters

    d) she loves her daughter

3. The time it takes a letter written in Lima to reach Madrid is:

    a) one month

    b) six months

    c) two months

    d) eight months

4. Doña Carla is always short of money because:

    a) Doña María sends her very little

    b) he husband has no money

    c) she spends heavily on gambling

    d) she gives money to artists and scientists

5. Doña María sends the King of Spain:

    a) a gold chain

    b) a Velasquez

    c) a Titian

    d) medicinal gum

6. When the Perichole insults Doña María at the theater, the Viceroy insists that she go to the lady and apologize for all of the following reasons *except:*

    a) he fears the Perichole is being unfaithful to him
    b) he is a particular friend of Doña María
    c) Doña María is a member of the Peruvian aristocracy
    d) Doña María's son-in-law is influential at the Spanish court

7. During her visit to Doña María, the Perichole feels the following emotion most strongly:

    a) contempt
    b) shame
    c) anger
    d) love

8. What are the plans of the Abbess for Pepita?

    a) for her to become a nun
    b) for her to marry well
    c) for her to become Abbess one day
    d) for her to serve a great lady

9. Doña María visits the shrine of Santa María de Cluxambuqua because:

    a) she is ill
    b) Pepita is ill
    c) Doña Clara is pregnant

10. On the day before her death Doña María reads:

    a) a letter from Pepita
    b) a letter from her daughter
    c) a letter from the Abbess
    d) a letter from her son-in-law

## Reading Quiz - Part Three: ESTEBAN

1. The twins come to the Convent of Santa María Rosa:

    a) having been found wandering the streets
    b) having been placed in the basket for unwanted babies at the convent
    c) having been taken away from their parents

2. The Abbess:

    a) comes to love the twins because she loves all men
    b) comes to love only one of the twins
    c) never feels any love for the twins
    d) loves the twins despite her dislike of men in general

3. Who attempts to study the secret language with which the twins communicate?

    a) the Archbishop
    b) the Viceroy
    c) the Abbess

4. Initially, the twins make their living as:

    a) painters
    b) cleaners
    c) scribes
    d) farm hands

5. Manuel first falls in 'love' with Camila Perichole when:

    a) working as a copyist at the theater, he sees her learning her lines
    b) he and his brother make their only visit to see a play at the theater
    c) she uses him to write letters to her two lovers
    d) she threatens to use Esteban to write letters for her

6. Manuel gives up his passion for Camila Perichole:

    a) before he injures his leg
    b) at the moment he injures his leg
    c) while Esteban is nursing him
    d) just before he dies

7. Esteban gets medical help for Manuel, but he dies:

    a) three hours later
    b) three days later
    c) three weeks later

8. Who suggests that Camila Perichole be brought to see Manuel?

    a) Manuel
    b) Esteban

9. For a time after his brother's death, Esteban uses the name Manuel. To whom does he first use his real name of Esteban?

    a) Madre María
    b) Camila Perichole
    c) Captain Alvarado

10. Captain Alvarado intends the voyage for which he recruits Esteban to be to:

    a) England and Russia
    b) Spain and Portugal
    c) Australia and New Zealand

11. For whom does Esteban intend to buy a present?

    a) Madre María
    b) Camila Perichole
    c) Captain Alvarado

## Reading Quiz - Part Four: UNCLE PIO

1. Uncle Pio runs away from home at age ten and spends his youth in:

    a) Lima
    b) Porto
    c) Madrid
    d) Lisbon

2. At age twenty, Uncle Pio's life is said to have three aims. Which of the following is *not* one of them?

    a) good literature
    b) good food
    c) independence
    d) beautiful women

3. Uncle Pio returns to Peru as a result of:

    a) a quarrel in a brothel
    b) his work for the Inquisition
    c) having many bad debts

4. Uncle Pio discovers Micaela Villegas singing in a café at the age of:

    a) ten
    b) eleven
    c) twelve
    d) thirteen

5. Camila Perichole becomes the mistress of:

    a) the Archbishop
    b) the Viceroy
    c) Captain Alvarado

6. Camila Perichole has how many illegitimate children?

    a) one
    b) two
    c) three
    d) four

7. Camila Perichole gives up acting:

    a) to raise her children
    b) because she gets small-pox
    c) to be a great lady

8. Uncle Pio succeeds in persuading her to let him take and educate Don Jamie for:

    a) one month
    b) six months
    c) one year
    d) five years

9. As they approach the bridge:

    a) Uncle Pio is carrying Don Jamie
    b) Don Jamie is riding in a cart
    c) Uncle Pio is holding Don Jamie's hand
    d) Uncle Pio is walking beside Don Jamie

## Reading Quiz - Part Five: PERHAPS AN INTENTION

1. Brother Juniper's friend, a master at the University of San Martín, is convinced that all is wrong with the world because his wife:

    a) ran off to go to a soldier
    b) died in child birth
    c) had small-pox
    d) ran away with a sailor

2. Brother Juniper sets about establishing "tabular proof

' that faith in God is justified by analyzing fifteen victims and fifteen survivors of:

    a) an earthquake
    b) an epidemic
    c) a tidal wave
    d) a volcanic eruption

3. His analysis of this data proves to Brother Juniper that those who died were:

    a) less worthy than the survivors
    b) neither more nor less worthy than the survivors
    c) more worthy than the survivors
    d) deserving of death

4. What happens to Brother Juniper's book:

    a) he tears it up and throws the bits into the sea
    b) he burns it
    c) it is confiscated
    d) it is burnt alongside him

5. Camila Perichole attends the memorial service for those killed in the bridge tragedy:

    a) true
    b) false

6. The Abbess attends the memorial service for those killed in the bridge tragedy:

    a) true
    b) false

7. The Captain attends the memorial service for those killed in the bridge tragedy:

    a) true
    b) false

8. The Viceroy attends the memorial service for those killed in the bridge tragedy:

    a) true
    b) false

9. Which of the following does not seek out the Abbess after the bridge tragedy?

    a) the Captain
    b) Camila Perichole
    c) Doña Carla

# Answers to Reading Quizzes

**Reading Quiz - Part One: PERHAPS AN ACCIDENT**
1. The Bridge of St. Louis Rey was built by: **c)**
2. The bridge carries: **c)**
3. The fall of the bridge is said to have impacted the behavior of all of the following *except*: **b)**
4. Brother Juniper is a monk of which order? **c)**
5. Brother Juniper's first thought when he sees the bridge collapse is, "Within ten minutes myself ..." **b)**
6. How many years does Brother Juniper spend compiling his book on the lives of the victims? **c)**
7. Which of the following is most accurate? **b)**

**Reading Quiz - Part Two: THE MARQUESA DE MONTEMAYOR**
1. Which of the following most accurately and completely reflects the view of the narrator? **c)**
2. The narrator calls Doña María a "wonderful woman" (14) for all of these reasons *except*: **a)**
3. The time it takes a letter written in Lima to reach Madrid is: **b)**
4. Doña Carla is always short of money because: **b)**
5. Doña María sends the King of Spain: **a)**
6. When the Perichole insults Doña María at the theater, the Viceroy insists that she go to the lady and apologize for all of the following reasons except: **b)**
7. During her visit to Doña María, the Perichole feels the following emotion most strongly: **b)**
8. What are the plans of the Abbess for Pepita? **c)**
9. Why does Doña María visits the shrine of Santa María de Cluxambuqua because: **c)**
10. On the day before her death Doña María reads: **a)**

**Reading Quiz - Part Three: ESTEBAN**
1. The twins come to the Convent of Santa María Rosa: **b)**
2. The Abbess: **d)**
3. Who attempts to study the secret language with which the twins communicate? **a)**
4. Initially, the twins make their living as: **c)**
5. Manuel first falls in 'love' with Camila Perichole when: **b)**
6. Manuel gives up his passion for Camila Perichole: **a)**

7. Esteban gets medical help for Manuel, but he dies: **b)**
8. Who suggests that Camila Perichole be brought to see Manuel? **b)**
9. For a time after his brother's death, Esteban uses the name Manuel. To whom does he first use his real name of Esteban? **c)**
10. Captain Alvarado intends the voyage for which he recruits Esteban to be to: **a)**
11. For whom does Esteban intend to buy a present? **a)**

## Reading Quiz - Part Four: UNCLE PIO

1. Uncle Pio runs away from home at age ten and spends his youth in: **d)**
2. At age twenty, Uncle Pio's life is said to have three aims. Which of the following is *not* one of them? **b)**
3. Uncle Pio returns to Peru as a result of: **a)**
4. Uncle Pio discovers Micaela Villegas singing in a café at the age of: **c)**
5. Camila Perichole becomes the mistress of: **c)**
6. Camila Perichole has how many illegitimate children? **c)**
7. Camila Perichole gives up acting: **c)**
8. Uncle Pio succeeds in persuading her to let him take and educate Don Jamie for: **c)**
9. As they approach the bridge: **a)**

## Reading Quiz - Part Five: PERHAPS AN INTENTION

1. Brother Juniper's friend, a master at the University of San Martín, is convinced that all is wrong with the world because his wife: **a)**
2. Brother Juniper sets about establishing "tabular proof" that faith in God is justified by analyzing fifteen victims and fifteen survivors of: **b)**
3. His analysis of this data proves to Brother Juniper that those who died were: **c)**
4. What happens to Brother Juniper's book: **d)**
5. Camila Perichole attends the memorial service for those killed in the bridge tragedy: **b)**
6. The Abbess attends the memorial service for those killed in the bridge tragedy: **a)**
7. The Captain attends the memorial service for those killed in the bridge tragedy: **b)**
8. The Viceroy attends the memorial service for those killed in the bridge tragedy: **a)**
9. Which of the following does *not* seek out the Abbess after the bridge tragedy? **a)**

41

# Graphic organizer: Plot

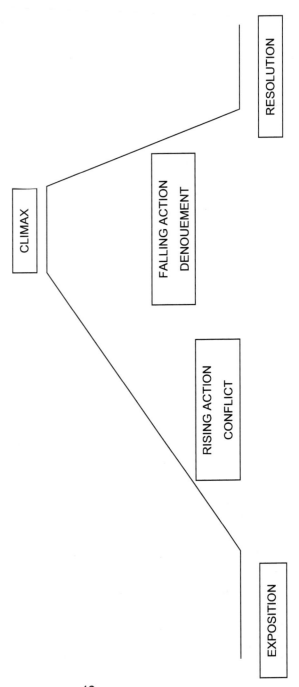

# Glossary of literary terms
## (useful in discussing this novel)

*first-person narrator/narrative* - The narrative in a work of fiction may either be third or first person. Third person narrative is told by an unidentified voice which belongs to someone not directly involved in the events narrated. First person narrative means that story is told from the necessarily limited viewpoint of one of the characters writing or speaking directly about themselves and their experience.

*foreshadowing* - An author uses foreshadowing when he/she hints at a future development in the plot. This builds up the reader's involvement in the fiction.

*image* - Imagery is a blanket term that describes the use of figurative language to represent objects, actions and ideas in such a way that it appeals to our five physical senses. Thus, amongst others, similes, metaphors and symbolism are examples of images.

> *metaphor* - A metaphor is a implied comparison in which whatever is being described is referred to as though it were another thing (e.g., "To be, or not to be: that is the question: / Whether 'tis nobler in the mind to suffer / The *slings and arrows* of outrageous *fortune*, / Or to take arms against *a sea of troubles*, / And by opposing end them?" Shakespeare *Hamlet*)

> *simile* - A simile is a descriptive comparison which uses the words "like" or "as" to make the intended comparison clear (e.g., "O my Luve's like a red, red rose / That's newly sprung in June; / O my Luve's like the melodie / That's sweetly play'd in tune." Robert Burns).

> *symbol* - A description in which one thing stand for or represents or suggests something bigger and more significant than itself. Normally a material object is used to represent an idea, belief, action, theme, person, etc. (e.g., in the Burns poem above, he uses the rose because it is a traditional symbol for love, passion, emotion and romance just as the sun became a natural and almost universal symbol of kingship).

*irony / ironic* - The essential feature of irony is the presence of a contradiction between an action or expression and the meaning it has in the context in which it occurs. Writers are always conscious of using irony, but there characters may either be aware or unaware that something that they say or do is ironic. Dramatic irony is the term used to describe a character saying or doing something that has significance for the audience or reader but of which the characters are not aware. For example, when Othello says, "If it were now to die, / 'Twere now to be most happy, for I fear / My soul hath her content so absolute / That not another comfort like to this / Succeeds in unknown fate" (*Othello* 2:1), this is dramatic irony because the audience knows that he speaks truer than he knows.

***motivation*** - Since Sigmund Freud 'invented' psychoanalysis, motivation has predominantly been though or in terms of psychology. Thus, the actions of a character may surprise us but they should also strike us as psychologically plausible.

# Appendix: Classroom Use of the Study Guide Questions

Although there are both closed and open questions in the Study Guide, very few of them have simple, right or wrong answers. They are designed to encourage in-depth discussion, disagreement, and (eventually) consensus. Above all, they aim to encourage students to go to the text to support their conclusions and interpretations.

I am not so arrogant as to presume to tell teachers how they should use this resource. I used it in the following ways, each of which ensured that students were well prepared for class discussion and presentations.

**1.** Set a reading assignment for the class and tell everyone to be aware that the questions will be the focus of whole class discussion the next class.

**2.** Set a reading assignment for the class and allocate particular questions to sections of the class (e.g. if there are four questions, divide the class into four sections, etc.).
In class, form discussion groups containing one person who has prepared each question and allow time for feedback within the groups.
Have feedback to the whole class on each question by picking a group at random to present their answers and to follow up with class discussion.

**3.** Set a reading assignment for the class, but do not allocate questions.
In class, divide students into groups and allocate to each group one of the questions related to the reading assignment the answer to which they will have to present formally to the class.
Allow time for discussion and preparation.

**4.** Set a reading assignment for the class, but do not allocate questions.
In class, divide students into groups and allocate to each group one of the questions related to the reading assignment.
Allow time for discussion and preparation.
Now reconfigure the groups so that each group contains at least one person who has prepared each question and allow time for feedback within the groups.

**5.** Before starting to read the text, allocate specific questions to individuals or pairs. (It is best not to allocate all questions to allow for other approaches and variety. One in three questions or one in four seems about right.) Tell students that they will be leading the class discussion on their question. They will need to start with a brief presentation of the issued and then conduct question and answer. After this, they will be expected to present a brief review of the discussion.

**6.** Having finished the text, arrange the class into groups of 3, 4 or 5. Tell each group to select as many questions from the Study Guide as there are members of the group.

Each individual is responsible for drafting out a written answer to one question, and each answer should be a substantial paragraph.

Each group as a whole is then responsible for discussing, editing and suggesting improvements to each answer, which is revised by the original writer and brought back to the group for a final proof reading followed by revision.

This seems to work best when the group knows that at least some of the points for the activity will be based on the quality of all of the answers

# To the Reader

Ray strives to make his products the best that they can be. If you have any comments or questions about this book *please* contact the author through his email: **moore.ray1@yahoo.com**
Visit his website at **http://www.raymooreauthor.com**
**Also by Ray Moore:** Most books are available from amazon.com as paperbacks and at most online eBook retailers.

## Fiction:

***The Lyle Thorne Mysteries:*** each book features five tales from the Golden Age of Detection:

*Investigations of The Reverend Lyle Thorne*
*Further Investigations of The Reverend Lyle Thorne*
*Early Investigations of Lyle Thorne*
*Sanditon Investigations of The Reverend Lyle Thorne*
*Final Investigations of The Reverend Lyle Thorne*

## Non-fiction:

The ***Critical Introduction series*** is written for high school teachers and students and for college undergraduates. Each volume gives an in-depth analysis of a key text:

*"The Stranger" by Albert Camus: A Critical Introduction* (Revised Second Edition)
*"The General Prologue" by Geoffrey Chaucer: A Critical Introduction*
*"Pride and Prejudice" by Jane Austen: A Critical Introduction*
*"The Great Gatsby" by F. Scott Fitzgerald: A Critical Introduction*

***The Text and Critical Introduction series*** differs from the Critical introduction series as these books contain the original text and in the case of the medieval texts an interlinear translation to aid the understanding of the text. The commentary allows the reader to develop a deeper understanding of the text and themes within the text.

*"Sir Gawain and the Green Knight": Text and Critical Introduction*
*"The General Prologue" by Geoffrey Chaucer: Text and Critical Introduction*
*"The Wife of Bath's Prologue and Tale" by Geoffrey Chaucer: Text and Critical Introduction*
*"Heart of Darkness" by Joseph Conrad: Text and Critical Introduction*
*"The Sign of Four" by Sir Arthur Conan Doyle Text and Critical Introduction*
*"A Room with a View" By E.M. Forster: Text and Critical Introduction*
*"Oedipus Rex" by Sophocles: Text and Critical Introduction*

**Study guides available in print- listed alphabetically by author**
    * *denotes also available as an eBook*

# A Study Guide

*"ME and EARL and the Dying GIRL" by Jesse Andrews: A Study Guide*
*"Wuthering Heights" by Emily Brontë: A Study Guide* *
*"Jane Eyre" by Charlotte Brontë: A Study Guide* *
*"The Myth of Sisyphus" and "The Stranger" by Albert Camus: Two Study Guides* *
*"The Meursault Investigation" by Kamel Daoud: A Study Guide*
*"Great Expectations" by Charles Dickens: A Study Guide* *
*"The Sign of Four" by Sir Arthur Conan Doyle: A Study Guide* *
*"A Room with a View" by E. M. Forster: A Study Guide*
*"Looking for Alaska" by John Green: A Study Guide*
*"Paper Towns" by John Green: A Study Guide*
*"Unbroken" by Laura Hillenbrand: A Study Guide*
*"The Kite Runner" by Khaled Hosseini: A Study Guide*
*"A Thousand Splendid Suns" by Khaled Hosseini: A Study Guide*
*"Go Set a Watchman" by Harper Lee: A Study Guide*
*"On the Road" by Jack Keruoac: A Study Guide*
*"The Secret Life of Bees" by Sue Monk Kidd: A Study Guide*
*"An Inspector Calls" by J.B. Priestley: A Study Guide*
*"The Catcher in the Rye" by J.D. Salinger: A Study Guide*
*"Macbeth" by William Shakespeare: A Study Guide* *
*"Othello" by William Shakespeare: A Study Guide* *
*"Antigone" by Sophocles: A Study Guide* *
*"Oedipus Rex" by Sophocles: A Study Guide*
*"Cannery Row" by John Steinbeck: A Study Guide*
*"East of Eden" by John Steinbeck: A Study Guide*
*"Of Mice and Men" by John Steinbeck: A Study Guide* *

**Study Guides available as e-books:**
*"Heart of Darkness" by Joseph Conrad: A Study Guide*
*"The Mill on the Floss" by George Eliot: A Study Guide*
*"Lord of the Flies" by William Golding: A Study Guide*
*"Catch-22" by Joseph Heller: A Study Guide*
*"Life of Pi" by Yann Martel: A Study Guide*
*"Nineteen Eighty-Four by George Orwell: A Study Guide*
*"Selected Poems" by Sylvia Plath: A Study Guide*
*"Henry IV Part 2" by William Shakespeare: A Study Guide*
*"Julius Caesar" by William Shakespeare: A Study Guide*
*"The Pearl" by John Steinbeck: A Study Guide*
*"Slaughterhouse-Five" by Kurt Vonnegut: A Study Guide*
*"The Bridge of San Luis Rey" by Thornton Wilder: A Study Guide*

**Teacher resources:** Ray also publishes many more study guides and other resources for classroom use on the 'Teachers Pay Teachers' website:
**http://www.teacherspayteachers.com/Store/Raymond-Moore**

Made in the USA
San Bernardino, CA
23 November 2019

60331152R10031